ISLAMABAD TODAY

Islamabad Today

The regime imagines the new capital as a symbolic theater of national ideology.

PRESIDENT FIELD MARSHAL MOHAMMAD AYUB KHAN
HITTING THE BALL TO INAUGURATE THE ISLAMABAD
GOLF COURSE ON NOVEMBER 5, 1967

ISLAMABAD TODAY

Issue No. 1 January 1968

Published by: **Public Relations Directorate,
Capital Development Authority, Rawalpindi.**
Edited by Maj. ZAMIR JAFRI.

THE NEW C.D.A. CHIEF

Lt Gen K. M. Sheikh has a long and distinguished record of public service in varied fields.

Born in Lahore in 1910, he was educated at the Government College, Lahore. A Sandhurst graduate, he was commissioned to the Army in 1932. Gen. Sheikh held various important command and staff posts in the Army. He was appointed Chief of General Staff in 1949. He attended the Imperial Defence College in 1950-51.

Gen. Sheikh represented Pakistan at several international conferences. In October, 1958 he became Minister in the Presidential Cabinet and was given portfolios of Home and State and Frontier Regions. He was also a member of the Economic Committee of the Cabinet. From 1960 to 1962 he was Minister-in-Charge of Food, Agriculture and Works.

In June, 1962 he was appointed Ambassador of Pakistan in Japan from where he went to Turkey in March, 1966.

THIS is the first issue of "Islamabad Today" which is proposed to be a bi-annual publication of the Capital Development Authority. The construction of the new Capital City is a history-making process. The aim is to provide information about the various aspects of this project. Our endeavour would be to narrate this great creative story, in pieces, as it unfolds itself.

Islamabad is growing in all dimensions. It now stretches itself to a considerable extent in each direction. A placid, low skyline of the new growing city is punctuated by tall office blocks and cleanly styled homes, set among lawns and young trees, against the backdrop of Margalla hills.

A new pattern of social life is fast taking shape. Within the large urban society are many, smaller, inter-related communities. The city has been planned in a way that every resident is a member of a closely knitted community of an easily manageable size thereby maintaining a comfortable living in an intimate neighbourhood, within the huge complex of a Capital city.

With a view to explaining the necessary background, basic concepts and image of the new city, we have included an article captioned as "The Project and Perspective" by Mr. N.A. Faruqui, who was Chairman of the Capital Development Authority from May 1, 1965 to November 30, 1967.

○ ○ ○

On the appointment of Mr. Faruqui, as the Chief Election Commissioner, Lt.-Gen. K.M. Sheikh took over as Chairman, Capital Development Authority on Dec. 30, 1967.

⊙ ○ ○

Earlier, in January 1967, Mian Manzoor Mohammad, Member Administration, CDA was posted as Joint Secretary, Home Affairs. Col. Muhammad Nawaz Khan succeeded him in February, 1967.

"THE PROJECT AND PERSPECTIVE"

By Mr. N.A. Faruqui, h.q.a., s.pk., c.s.p.
Former Chairman, C.D.A.

It is just over six years, when the first spade was struck in 1961 to lay the foundations of Islamabad, the national capital of Pakistan. Naturally, there are yet vast gaps which require lot of hard work and imagination to fill up, but the city of the future has emerged into the present, in certain outlines. In the past few brief years, Islamabad's population has risen to nearly 50,000 spread over three residential sectors, each covering one-and-a-quarter square mile area. More than half of the central administration is already functioning from the new Capital.

The stage has now been reached when the initiative is beginning to shift to the private sector which is getting into stride. About 1,000 private houses, including commercial and medium-size industrial establishments, have already come up.

The Design Committee for Islamabad public buildings scrutinizing design of the Plan House and Ministry of Defence block at the C.D.A. Headquarters. Photo shows from (left to right) Mr. I.A. Khan, Secretary, Economic Affairs; Mr. M.H. Sufi, Works Secretary; Mr. Ghiasuddin Ahmad, Defence Secretary; Mr. M.M. Ahmad, Deputy Chairman, Planning Commission; Mr. N.A. Faruqui, Chairman, C.D.A., and Mr. Qamrul Islam, Secretary, Planning Division. On extreme left is Mr. Rosselli, the architect.

A view of the four Blocks of Secretariat Buildings housing offices of the Central Government.

It must exemplify the modern centralized state as a concrete symbol of a progressive and Islamic society.

BACKGROUND

The story of Islamabad, however, goes back to 1947. It is, in fact, a story of the national urge for self-expression.

The new sovereign State of Pakistan came into being on August 14, 1947, within few weeks of the initial announcement by Great Britain. The Central Government of the new State, therefore, had to be hurriedly shifted from Delhi to somewhere in Pakistan and, under the circumstances, Karachi was then the only city where it could go. It was, however, a purely temporary arrangement to establish a bridge-head. The need to have a proper capital was in the mind of the people and the Government ever since the inception of Pakistan. The Central Government had no permanent home of its own.

Though a new country we, as a people, are an old nation, with a rich heritage. Inspired by a historical past, and keen to build a dignified present and a great future, the people naturally were eager to build a new city which, in addition to being an adequate and ideal seat of government, should also reflect our cultural identity and

3

The project for the capital is entrusted to Constantinos Doxiadis, known for his theorization of the science of settlements known as Ekistics.

Children's Park in the Model School.

national aspirations. "The Capital of a Country", to quote President Ayub Khan, "has to encompass much bigger vistas and provide light and direction to the efforts of the people. It must, therefore, be located in the best possible surroundings".

The image visualised was to have ideal environments for the location of the all-important Central Government, which is also a focal point for administrative, political and cultural institutions. The national capital has to be a 'leader of cities'. Islamabad has been conceived and planned and is now being built in that spirit.

The proposal to erect a new capital city was in the thoughts of the successive governments. Several locations were studied, and even one or two selected, but the project could not be pursued determinedly. In 1958 when President Ayub Khan came to the helm, and the country achieved political stability and economic progress, this important national task became practical politics.

In February 1959 a Site Selection Commission was appointed to consider the suitability of Karachi, as the capital, from the point of view of location, climate, availability of adequate water and food supply, communications and defence: and,

4

if Karachi was unsuitable, to recommend another site. After comprehensive surveys of all possibilities, the Commission unanimously recommended the terraced table-land of the Potwar plateau, near Rawalpindi. In June 1959 the Government accepted the recommendations of the Commission and took the historic decision to build the national capital which was, later, named Islamabad-the city of Islam. This closed the chapter of our transit camp mentality.

The Federal Capital Commission was formed in September 1959 to produce a Master Plan. The Master Plan, prepared in October 1960, fixed the location of the site, its size in successive stages of development and its relation with the surrounding areas, and divided it into various sectors. This marked the start of a race against time.

The agency entrusted with the gigantic task of building Islamabad, the Capital Development Authority, came into being on September 8, 1960. The general direction and administration of the Authority, and its affairs, vest in a Board which is required to act on sound principles of development, town planning and housing. On question of policy, the Central Govt. may issue directives from time to time.

NO REFLECTION ON KARACHI

The selection of a new site implies no reflection on Karachi as a town. Karachi is a mighty city and its importance is inherent in its geographical position and industrial and commercial importance. It will always remain a great port, a vital air route and a great terminus for the flow of commerce and industry. As Pakistan grows, so will Karachi. With the shifting of the capital it will assume, no doubt, a character of its own nearer to its more normal and natural functions. Karachi is a city with a great future.

Office Buildings in Sector G-6

Moghul - style garden of the Secretariat Buildings 'B' Block.

NEW SITE

However, the piece of land chosen for the capital has an undisputable claim to the honour bestowed upon it. History and legend have combined to lend an ageless charm and an undying soul to the site. Spreading over an area of 351 square miles, it is a panoramic expanse of natural terraces and meadows rising from 1700 to 2000 feet above sea level. It is traversed by mountain torrents which flow down, during the well-distributed rains, from the 5000 feet high Margalla range in the north. The lofty lush green Murree hills offer a pleasant vista on one side. Nearby towards the west lie the historic ruins of fabled Taxila, cradle of the celebrated Gandhara civilization.

Sheltered by the northern hills, the area is strategically safe, scenically beautiful, and climatically pleasant and bracing almost the whole year round. And it is rich in building materials. It is hard to think of a site so richly endowed by Nature and so convenient for man to build up a beautiful and dynamic city. Being located in close proximity to the existing Rawalpindi city, Islamabad will have the additional advantage of utilising facilities and services available at Rawalpindi.

Main Mosque in the Class **V** Centre of Sector G-6

MOBILE PLAN

The urbanisation of Islamabad is based on the principle of 'dynapolis', that is to say, a mobile arrangement which grows in scale and size smoothly and coherently with all the functions of city life, at all stages of development, the city-centre moving proportionately to the movement of the residential sectors.

Each sector is a self-contained township, satisfying all needs. While it takes care of all the requirements of modernity, it ensures at the same time the traditional character of the neighbourhood, serving the residents at the human level and enabling them to live comfortably in happier surroundings. There is no discrimination in the matter of services and facilities. Unity of the city as a whole would be achieved through detailed zoning regulations, framed to exercise control on town-planning and architecture.

FUNCTIONAL ZONES

The city is divided into various functional zones which broadly are:—

(*i*) **The Administrative Sector**

This sector is located towards the north-east and is situated on the main axis of the city. It will contain the principal public buildings like the

7

The first group of experts from Doxiadis Associates reaches Rawalpindi in November 1959 and undertakes a process of systematic data collection.

President's House, the Secretariat blocks, the National Assembly building, the Supreme Court and a group of cultural buildings. It would form the most focal complex of the metropolitan city. This sector has already come to life with the shifting of the Ministries to the permanent Secretariat buildings. The Central Square---the heart of Islamabad—comprising the National Assembly building, the President's House, the Foreign Office and Cabinet Division block is expected to start throbbing by 1970.

Alongwith the Central Square, the CDA also hopes to complete the Plan House—headquarters of the Planning Commission—which would be so situated as to form the hub of the massive Secretariat blocks.

A view of the Poly - Clinic in Sector G-6

(ii) The Diplomatic Enclave

The special enclave for the chanceries and residences of the foreign missions is situated in a very pleasant setting, close to the picturesque Rawal lake. With an average elevation of 1800 feet above sea level, its gentle slopes lend themselves to the construction of interesting buildings at various levels. A small stream meanders through the area.

(iii) The Residential Sectors

The residential sectors have been planned in rows, placed on both sides of the main civic, commerce and business centre which runs in the heart of the town. The area of each residential sector is 1.25 square miles and

8

the plots vary in size from 600 to 2,000 square yards. Each sector is, in itself, a self-contained and self-sufficient township. A sector is again sub-divided into several smaller residential neighbourhoods which are served by various grades of community centres, equipped with civic facilities and services like schools, mosques, markets, dispensaries, play-grounds, parks, etc., according to their requirements. The main community centre of a sector will have offices for local services, higher educational institutions, the sectoral post office, hospital, police station, cinema house, club and large departmental shops and store houses. This civic hierarchy is repeated more or less in each sector. The emphasis has been on the provision of facilities and services almost at the doorstep.

(*iv*) **The National Park**

A vast valley is earmarked as the National Park area mainly for academic and recreational purposes. The area would have institutions of national importance such as the Atomic Research Institute, the National Health Centre and a spacious sports centre including an Olympic Village.

Moghul - style garden in the five - wing Government Hostel

The Shahinshah of Iran planting a sapling at the Shakarparian Hill Garden during a visit to Islamabad on March 7, 67. Also seen in the picture are President Field Marshal Mohammad Ayub Khan and Queen Farah Pehlavi.

The President of Turkey, General Cevdet Su accompanied by President Field Marshal Moham Ayub Khan, arriving at the Shakarparian Hill Ga to have a panoramic view of the new Capital.

...ent Field Marshal Mohammad Ayub Khan ...ning the architectural feature of the Government ... to King Faisal of Saudi Arabia, during the ... visit to Islamabad.

King Hussein of Jordan seen at the Secretariat Buildings during a visit to Islamabad on September 21, 1967. Also seen with the King is President Field Marshal Mohammad Ayub Khan.

A view of the fast developing City.

In February 1960, Ayub Khan and his government choose the name Islamabad for the capital from a shortlist which also includes Ayubabad, Muslimabad, and Jinnahpur.

Interior of the main Mosque in the Class V Centre of Sector G-6.

Post Office building in the Class V Centre of Sector G-6.

PROGRESS AT A GLANCE

WORKS.	PROGRESS UPTO 31-12-1967
1. **Acquisition of Land:**	44,408 acres.
2. **Rehabilitation of Displaced Families:**	7,709 families on 1,12,560 acres of land in Sahiwal, Multan and Guddu Barrage areas.
3. **Office Accommodation:**	
(*i*) Office Blocks.	6 Office Blocks, functioning in Sector G6-V.
(*ii*) Facade Block.	Completed.
(*iii*) Secretariat Buildings Phase-I.	Completed and occupied by ten Ministries/ Divisions of the Central Secretariat.
(*iv*) Secretariat Buildings Phase-II.	Three blocks nearing completion for occupation. One block completed and occupied by the Ministry of Finance.
4. **Hotel Shahrazad:** (275-room hotel).	Functioning.
5. **Government Hostel:** (168 rooms).	Functioning.

16

The territory of the capital, which includes both Islamabad and Rawalpindi, covers an area of a thousand square kilometers. The lands are purchased in 1960 from the provinces of Punjab and the North-West Frontier.

6. **Houses:**

    (*i*) A to I types houses.   6,219 houses completed.

    (*ii*) 5 'G' type houses.   Nearing completion.

    (*iii*) 1,371 (A to D type houses).   Under construction.

7. **Roads:**   (All grades).   Over 125 miles completed.

8. **Bridges:**   (All grades).   About 125 bridges constructed.

9. **Water Supply:**   Present water supply 14 million gallons per day.

10. **Bulk Water Supply Phase-1:**

    (*i*) Conduction Main.

    (*ii*) Filteration Plant.   Work in progress. Additional 24 m.g.d. would be supplied after commissioning of the Simly Dam.

    (*iii*) Diversion Tunnel.

Government Printing Press

Gumrah River Bridge on the National Park Road

11. **Sewerage System:**

    (*i*) Sewage Treatment Plant.   One plant completed.

    (*ii*) Trunk Sewer.   Completed.

    (*iii*) Internal sewer net work.   Work in Progress.

12. **Drainage System:**   Work in progress.

13. **Landscaping :**

    (*i*) A nursery on 35 acres.   Developed.

    (*ii*) Afforestation, Horticulture   About 13 lacs plants have so far been
       and Arboriculture.   planted over 20,350 acres.

14. **Commercial Centres:**

    (*i*) 2 Food Markets.

    (*ii*) One Covered Bazar   } Completed.

    (*iii*) 5 Class III Shopping Centres

An office in the new Secretariat Buildings.

A small mosque in the Class III Centre of residential Sector G-7.

(*iv*) 58 Shops and flats. }

(*v*) Shops and Restaurant. } Completed.

(*iv*) 6 Class III shopping Centres.   Under construction.

15. Mosques:

(*i*) 4 Mosques each for 350 persons. ⎫

(*ii*) 1 Mosque for 1000 persons. ⎬ 5 mosques completed.

(*iii*) 1 Mosque for 2000 persons. ⎭

16. Educational Institutions:

(*i*) **Primary Schools.**

Six primary schools completed and are functioning.

One primary school is under construction and is nearing completion.

Schematic design of the Ministry of Defence Block.

(ii) **Secondary Schools.**	Four secondary schools completed and are functioning. (Out of these four schools, one school is Bengali-Medium)
	One secondary school is under construction and is nearing completion.
(iii) **Combined Schools.**	Islamabad Model School, functioning.
	Primary and Secondary School (Bengali Medium) functioning.
(iv) **Colleges.**	Girls Intermediate College (housed temporarily in a primary school building in Sector F6-4) functioning.
	Islamabad Boys Intermediate College in Sector H-9, functioning.
	Degree college for boys in Sector H-9, functioning.
17. **Inter-University Board Building in Sector H-9**:	Completed.
18. **Diplomatic Enclave:**	31 foreign missions have purchased 7,86,190 sq. yds of land for chanceries and residences.
19. **Primary Health Centre for Outdoor and indoor treatment:**	Functioning.

20

Two areas to the north and north-east of Rawalpindi are identified where issues of transportation and communications as well as factors of national interest and defence appear to converge.

Fire Headquarters building, under construction in Sector G-7.

20. **Cinema**:   Functioning.

21. **Post Office**:   Post offices functioning.

22. **Telephone and Telegraph**:   Main Telegraph Exchange functioning.

23. **Slaughter House**:   Under construction. ..

24. **Fire Headquarters**:   Under construction.

A TURNING POINT

The October Revolution of 1958 was a turning point in our national history, which marked the beginning of a new era of hope and confidence; of self-respect and self-expression. In less than a decade a vast transformation has taken place on the national scene. The progress in all directions has indeed been phenomenal. The country has come a long way on the road of prosperity under the dynamic and able leadership of President Field Marshal Mohammad Ayub Khan. The construction of Islamabad symbolises the spirit of this national reconstruction and creative activity.

Lt.-General K. M. Sheikh,
Chairman,
Capital Development Authority.

(*Continued from page* 11)

Constant efforts are being made to introduce Islamic architecture, happily blended with the requirements of modern architecture. The architects have been asked to develop a new architecture of our own which, while being adapted to the present day conditions, reflects our great architectural heritage. As a result of these efforts, the desired effect has been achieved in the architecture of the Govt. Hostel, Fire Headquarters, Facade Block and the landscaping of the Secretariat Buildings. The latest design of the President's House depicts it more than ever.

CITY OF GARDENS

Few nations can claim to be the inheritors of such a rich tradition of gardening as the Pakistanis. Pakistan's new capital would be a city of gardens and open spaces. Meticulous attention is being given to the landscaping of Islamabad for recreational and aesthetic values. In Islamic architecture, free use was made of trees and water. So far as water is concerned, within the limitations that exist, it will be made use of. But the trees can and are being planted freely. About 14,00,000 trees have already been planted in the Capital Area, including the Islamabad face of the Margalla hill range, which forms a crescent—like backdrop to the city. Care has been taken that the pattern of landscaping should aesthetically conform to the general pattern of the layout and the architecture.

CONCLUSION

The building of a befitting capital is a project of great magnitude. There are numerous difficulties and limitations. But our great asset is the will and the vigour of the people, determined to forge ahead, with the help of Allah, under all circumstances.

The next step is therefore to design two bypasses of the Grand Trunk Road that cut around Rawalpindi to the north and south.

22

Inside a Shop in Aab Para Market.

melody
CINEMA – ISLAMABAD

A PRIDE PART
OF PRIDE
CAPITAL OF
PAKISTAN

ASIA'S MOST
LAVISHLY
ARTISTICALLY
DESIGNED

MELODY
(Air-Conditioned)
SHOW PIECE OF ISLAMABAD
equipped with 70 m.m. Projection - only of its kind in Northern Pakistan

PROVIDES BEFITTING ENTERTAINMENT
MODERN CONVENIENCES
—also inaugurating shortly—
MOST MODERN MAGNIFICENT AND ELEGANT
KEHKASHAN RESTAURANT
(AIR-CONDITIONED)

_____ & _____

Melody's Shopping Arcade
(ALL SHOPS AIR-CONDITIONED)

Owner: **MOHAMMED FAROOQ KHAN,**
Managing Director,
FAROOQ & KHAWAR LIMITED,
ISLAMABAD.

Phone: 21165, 21166   Cable: "MELODY"

The one to the north, the
Islamabad Highway, becomes
the border between the
new capital and the old city.

حبیب بنک

کے

۲۶ سال

بہترخدمت کی بہترین مثال

PRINTED AT FEROZSONS RAWALPINDI

VOICES FROM PAKISTAN
Paolo Rosselli

AHMED Z. KHAN

Paolo, I saw you've been trying to call me; sorry—
I often don't answer when I'm teaching, and then
when I get home I forget, you know how it is,
and what's more I don't like mobile phones, so often
I just ignore mine completely.

PAOLO ROSSELLI

Ahmed, at last! You just disappeared into thin air and I thought
you had packed your bags and moved elsewhere. I just wanted
to tell you it's time to set out on that journey to Islamabad...
You remember we talked about it? But in 2002 there was the
danger of war breaking out after September 11, and quite frankly
I really didn't feel like getting blown to bits...

AHMED Z. KHAN

Did I hear you right? Did you say it's time to leave?
And so you want to go and see what your father and
grandfather got up to, do you?

PAOLO ROSSELLI

Yeah, I'm getting sort of Pakistan fever, you know? Anyway,
speaking of war, tell me about what's going on at the moment
between India and Pakistan: is it real war? I've been following
events on NDTV, it's hard to tell what's really going on.

AHMED Z. KHAN

Nah, really, look, it's just Indian TV making a big
fuss. There's nothing going on, just Indian nation-
alism rearing its head thanks to Modi.

PAOLO ROSSELLI

OK so it's just the usual... The other evening I was trying to
follow a debate carefully, but at a certain point I moved over to
another "top story" because I was getting bored; they were all
on a knife edge about the 'complexity' of it all, but it was clear
that the whole debate was revolving around nothing. After all,
that's what the media do: they turn the banal into the incompre-
hensible, don't they? Are you going to Islamabad to visit your
family by any chance?

AHMED Z. KHAN

Yes, I'm going to visit my parents for three weeks at
Christmas. You try and arrive in the second week of
January 2020 so I can show you around, and remem-
ber I have to be back in Belgium on January 19.

PAOLO ROSSELLI

Sure, I'll look into it today and let you know. Ah, by the way,
there's two of us, I'm with a photographer friend who has a
book project in mind. She's called Giovanna Silva, I'll tell you
more another time.

AHMED Z. KHAN

Ah, wonderful; anyway, you start sending me the
scans of your passports and the rest of the paper
trail and then we'll be in touch.[1]

1
Phone conversation
with Ahmed Z. Khan,
professor at the Vrije
Universiteit in Brussels,
October 2019.

2
Constantinos Apostolou
Doxiadis, Greek
architect. In 1960 he
devised the urban layout
of Islamabad, as
commissioned by the
Pakistani government.

For hours we flew over a snow-capped Asia, and at the moment
we are soaring above the region of Islamabad, but the ten-mile-
long rectangle that hosts the city has yet to appear from among
the clouds; I know it by heart, having read of Constantinos
Doxiadis'[2] commission from the Pakistani government in 1960
to map out roads and blocks, swallowing up the tiny Lake Rawal.
As the plane descends, I explore the landscape, in search of
something to fix my gaze on, but there is still nothing if not
dirt tracks, a few little houses, and the odd buffalo wandering
around the fields. The airport is new and spacious. Outside,

our driver Ghassan is waiting for us, grinning and all wrapped up against the cold. More than the temperature being particularly low, the humidity is high: it's the dawn of February 4, 2020, and among the pilasters and suspended walkways, delicate shades of light blue and gray may be made out on the horizon. While Giovanna exchanges euro for rupees, I ask Ghassan for news of the high-speed railway line that should link China and Pakistan, which an Afghan friend who has long lived in Germany had been

telling me about. He looks at me: he knows nothing of it; indeed, he doesn't even believe it exists. But not wanting to let me down, he adds: "I have a Chinese wife, but now she's in Gilgit, the big city in the north." Good, a Chinese wife is even better, I congratulate him; and with Gilgit and his wife in mind, we get into Ghassan's ivory-toned Honda. Over the days to come, I would go back to the topic of the railway, receiving answers of various kinds, from the bizarre to the simply frustrating: "Yeah, it's being built. No, never heard of trains towards China. Yes, I've heard it exists but from Karachi. Could you imagine that? A railway line is impossible—they'd have to go through the Karakorum…"

Along the straight road that leads to the city, I notice the habit (like in India) of drifting across the four lanes, regardless of the traffic, and of stopping off at traffic lights to trade goods and have a quick chat with a glass of tea in hand. Quick note: I know India, having spent months in various years there, and I often find myself comparing the image of Pakistan with that of India in order to pick out differences and similarities. Since affinities go far beyond distances, I then find myself testing the ground, at dinner with architects and professors, saying that in my opinion, the partition of 1947 was not a great idea; the polite smiles lead me to think that, at the end of the day, perhaps they don't disagree with me so much. I have to admit that, making reference to 2020 Europe, politics is a "Propaganda Agency for Wrong Ideas," often run by fellows always ready to pick a fight, in cahoots with the mass media and always looking to make a quick buck. On hearing my tales of India, they reply that they have never been there, and that they feel a sense of nostalgia for their giant and inaccessible neighbor, home to their origins. This curious longing for something they have only imagined strikes me by virtue of the earnestness with which it is expressed. It is communicated to me with sincere and almost solemn words by Fauzia Asad Khan, president of the IAP,[3] over the course of one of the many car journeys in an afternoon marked by the yellow and reddish hues standing out against the deep blue-gray background of the sky. A capable woman,

3
IAP, Institute of
Architects Pakistan,
Islamabad.

one used to managing institutions with a firm hand, she ended up on the blacklist of figures disapproved of by the Indian government merely due to her being the daughter of a general in the Pakistani army. And slowly, this nostalgia for something unknown starts to catch on and infect me too; clearly even in my own little world, I have my accounts to settle.

Shortly before leaving, I had begun *Empires of the Indus* by Alice Albinia[4] which, in a tale midway between reality, history, and imagination, made me think how the journey to Pakistan, to the source of the Indus that it describes, is at times not exactly invented but I might say dreamt. Albinia herself seems to be possessed by the desire to grasp something that doesn't exist: a nostalgia for something which is out of reach, a personal issue between her, the Indus, Alexander the Great, the colonial period, and modern-day Pakistan, shaken by political-tribal-terroristic fevers. On the other hand, as a highly informed journalist who spent years "in a sweltering attic in Delhi,"[5] she reports that Muhammad Ali Jinnah,[6] the father of the nation, after being given the state of Pakistan, proved unable to shape the new nation. Or perhaps he realized that he didn't even want to, being himself a man of British education, and thus a blend of aristocratic detachment and skepticism. In Albinia's book, he may be seen caressing two dogs in his garden at sunset, the long shadows cast by the photographer and his assistant creeping into the image. One evening, I also decided to try my hand at journalism, asking my Pakistani (by now) friends to tell me about Abbottabad, the town some forty kilometers from Islamabad where Osama Bin Laden was executed by the CIA. But from the reactions, I sensed I had plucked the wrong strings and that the topic is still too much of a sore point.

After following about six miles of straight road, a long curve brings us into the neighborhood where we will be staying for five nights. On the roadside lies a block of colored concrete, which most likely actually did fall off the back of a truck; I memorize it as a form of street sign, and over the days to come, that yellowish orange of the concrete would be the sign announcing we were nearly home. But from the car window,

4
Alice Albinia, *Empires of the Indus: the Story of a River* (London: John Murray 2008).

5
Ibid, p. 15.

6
Muhammad Ali Jinnah, first governor of Pakistan, 1876–1948.

we also witness other marvels, like the sequence of residential buildings along the road which follows a curious progression: the first in any series is minimalist and serves as a model; the second maintains the structure but already shows a number of frills beyond the strictly necessary; the third building goes even further, also featuring a number of vernacular elements; while in the fourth and fifth, an Asiatic-European style explodes with fireplaces, convoluted portals, gateways, and barbed wire along the tops of the walls. Amid the eucalyptuses, we may also make out other brick buildings which are not bad at all—property to be bought up immediately, my traveling companion suggests. And on this topic, we two Italians would go on to entertain ourselves regularly: one thinking of a villa with a garden, a cook, and a driver; the other rambling about occupying an entire floor of the Secretariat Building as an inalienable right of the designer's son.

Writers, or the precious few of them who still go to see a country in person, do not shy away from the little troubles that transform even the most dramatic reality into a ridiculous puzzle: this may range from the door that won't open to food with a dubious flavor to the waiter whose jacket sports coffee stains. And then there are the broken lifts, the offices full of demotivated employees, typical fallout of contemporary revolutions when, flying in the face of all logic, they are actually translated into something concrete. The chapter on wrong addresses is a topic in its own right. There is something truly comical about setting out to photograph a building, convinced that it's the right one, only to realize that the name alone is "right." And it must have happened to others before us as well, yet ones who failed to then report the episode out of a sense of shame. Here is the tale of one such event.

Scene No. 1, 10:15 am. In a certain street, a building might even look like one designed by Gio Ponti, but only in terms of size and number of floors (five), featuring loggias on the street side. And, if we wish to believe our local guides (they too somewhat embarrassed in comparing the dingy light-gray parallelepiped with the photograph taken at the time), it actually is his work, just sixty years down the line. Fair enough, back in the day it was quite something else, but the new owner, "an unscrupulous fellow," has altered the building quite radically: alas, thus is the way of the "globalized and capitalist" world. From the terrace, a little forlorn and troubled by the loss of such a piece of architecture, we find consolation in the background of mountains cited by Alberto Rosselli in his reports on the Secretariats, published in *National Geographic* as far back as 1967: "The nature of the place with the outline of the mountains in the background turned out to be a decisive factor in finding the right setting for the architecture. The buildings were placed on the ground at various levels, avoiding any upheaval of nature."[7] The green mountains stayed there, but a whole city was built up around them, albeit one of a low density by Asian standards.

Scene No. 2, 12:15 pm. In just a few minutes, what we had by then given up on actually happened. Rather, after two hours of hellish torture, we are given the key to paradise: Salman Javaid Malik, a very punctilious architect and one with a good memory (from that moment on elected our guardian angel), asks if he can see the photograph of the original building once more. He shakes his head; something is not right. He checks his iPhone and immediately hits the spot: the right building is four blocks further west, hidden by the trees and in perfect condition, he's quite sure of it. There is widespread consolation and gratitude at this discovery, and a pleasant sense of relief spreads through us. But as I get back into the car, I cannot deny that however much the story has a happy ending, I am still quite disturbed by just how easy it is to be taken in by a wrong address. By this point, we have compiled quite a series of photos of kitsch stuccos, stairs and bannisters, armchairs in fake leather: what are we going to do with them? And so we decide to make

7
Alberto Rosselli, report on the buildings of Islamabad, 1968, Alberto Rosselli Archive, Milan.

our mistake public, even at the cost of making ourselves look silly. So once more, the caravan of cars makes its way towards the building in question which, as chance would have it, is not far from our hotel—the Serai, previously home to the Bulgarian embassy, complete with commemorative plaque at the entrance.

It's basically a pleasant hotel with two rooms, occupied by us two Italians: television on from seven in the morning, inscrutable guests, and a reception comprising two guys dressed European style, forever crouching over their laptops.

On finally visiting the ex-Hotel Sheherazade, today the Foreign Ministry, the emblems of Ponti's work emerge in the midst of local and not-so-Islamic elements (the semi-laicity of the Pakistani state of the 1960s has remained: no cupolas or minaret towers reaching skywards) but domestic ones, such as flowerboxes, tiles, plant pots, and hedges, meticulously placed three meters apart from one another. The civil servants pass the scanners and enter; in the square, dark and shiny cars wait with their doors open. Just in this moment, a minister is coming out, and his driver, half asleep, comes back to life; the blue Kia sets off once more for another destination, while the military men in green camouflage gear vigorously salute as he passes. A guy peers down from one of those balconies with Ponti's rounded corners—"stay still, please"—but he's not convinced and quickly moves back inside. Over the two hours, we are free to photograph no more than the outside and under surveillance, albeit with great politeness. The guy with the beige jacket and light-blue trousers serves as a guide and even leads us round to the back, eying every move we make. On the walls, we see the typical Ponti treatment with egg-shaped cobblestones applied to the facades, imported directly from Milan.

In all the excitement, I just manage to notice that the building displays a number of similarities with certain architectural works by Ponti in Italy: the curved walls, hints of pinnacles, elements vaguely reminiscent of church facades, although Ponti's churches are buildings that rather bring to mind lightweight Japanese origami given solid form. After leading us around and even showing us the entrance hall for exactly four minutes, our guide takes his leave with a handshake. He's sorry to go but he has things to do today. We find our car once more in the never-ending parking lot, say goodbye to the security guards, who by this point know everything about us (Italy, parents, grandparents, the fabulous 1960s), and make our way onto Constitution Avenue, which in the meantime has been cut down to a single lane for routine checks; today the police are in a good mood or simply bored: a quick glance to make sure the passengers look trustworthy followed by an Indian-style manual signal (rapid hand rotation from the wrist) telling us to proceed.

But stress is indeed a key component of any travel in Pakistan, and it was to reach its highest level just a few days later in the attempt to access the Secretariat Buildings designed by

Rosselli, sealed off inside an impenetrable red zone. After much moving around and various attempts at access, by the very purest of chance (Salman's cousin knows a security agent whom he defines as a friend, who then turns up a short while later to escort us in a bulletproof dark green Toyota), we reach the Italian embassy. And here the intervention of Stefano Pontecorvo (whose enigmatic response to my my question "Ambassador, are you by any chance related to the director?" even cited the naturalized Soviet scientist, yet leaving me in doubt as to any actual blood ties, although I would have never taken issue with the scientist's clamorous defection to the Eastern Bloc) elegantly solves the problem with a WhatsApp phone call to his friend, the director of the department of economics or agriculture or theater studies, I don't remember. As we get back into the car, a *carabiniere* born in Bolzano takes me aside and suggests I should view the River Indus as the real reason behind the tension between India and Pakistan. The name of the legendary river reached by Alexander the Great two thousand four hundred years earlier comes up again; Albinia's ferocious intuition, with all her wandering in search of its source, comes back into play.

In the area of the Secretariats, a series of L-shaped buildings laid out on a hill for almost a kilometer, I rediscover a style familiar to me (not in the sense of belonging to my family): detached yet not cold, and by no means bowing out to local styles. Rosselli writes: "As reference is made to the issue of the Islamic tradition with regard to the architecture of Islamabad, I would like to speak about nature and the misunderstandings that this may entail. We have never underestimated this theme, but rather we have always tried to separate it from such misunderstandings, rhetoric, and formalism. Tradition often constitutes a handy tool to sidestep the problems of one's own era—a procedure by which to obtain the consent of the authorities and the population alike. All the European peoples are steeped in tradition and they have all made their mistakes, the Italians first and foremost with the Roman tradition and all that entailed over the following centuries... As Western architects in the East, we have tried to define a manner in which to approach tradition, not in terms of forms of the past but of the environment as a whole, of culture, ways of living and the climate. We surpassed the rationalist ideology on the basis of an interpretation of the environment. But we had to maintain a rational approach before the issues of technology, of economics. [...] In Islamabad, numerous hypotheses and many alternatives immediately arose around the ministries program. On one hand, the European tradition provided us with examples of historical palazzos; on the other, contemporary architecture offered us examples of rationality more than anything else, of research bound by the principles of technological development. These elements aside, the local environment intervened to lead our attention towards other interests, the scale of the landscape, culture and tradition, the climate. Should the architect not be influenced? Should he not try to give an interpretation of it? This is perhaps a problem still unknown to the designer of industrial products, yet fundamental for the architect who has to operate in these countries. The architect cannot elude the more subtle issues of the relationships that exist between nature and architectural works, between the landscape and the urban fabric, of architecture midway between the human environment and the climate, midway between tradition and reality."[8] A message all too clear: as a boy I would see him writing on white sheets of paper of Japanese production—shorter than A4s—with a black Aurora. One day he put me on my guard: "You and I have something in common: we forever feel obliged to be ready." An enigmatic sentence (did he mean "you will have a life full of commitments?") yet one committed to memory, for the lessons imparted to his twelve-year-old son were few and far between.

We move quickly as we take our shots (almost three hours available here because they are about to close and the following day, Saturday, it's all closed) amid white buildings ten storeys high, gardens, brick stairways dotted with girls staring at their mobile phones; on the lawn there are men praying, a scene lit up by the afternoon sun of half past three. Up above, on the top three floors of the Secretariats, a vertical column (or a premeditated angle) of bow windows look west, endowing the final part of the building—usually windowless—with new

8
Alberto Rosselli, report on the Islamabad project, 1966, Alberto Rosselli Archive, Milan.

meaning. Unable to see for myself (I'm forbidden from going up) I imagine that from these westward openings the plain may be seen, along with the city right up to Lake Rawal and, in the background, Rawalpindi shrouded in the mist. I stop and gather the images memorized over decades of staring absorbedly at his works: it appears that even here in Islamabad, Rosselli's fixation with windows and openings emerges. Something similar may be found in the Swiss, Ligurian, and Piedmontese houses he designed—and which are still standing—that are systematically broken up by internal windows that bind the space together in visual terms; or even in the house in Via Rovani in Milan: noble but ultimately boring, with such thick supporting walls as to veritably invite you to cut right into them or knock them through in order for the light to reflect off the white walls.

Exhausted after working, we all head for the canteen of the Secretariats, where I toast with water to my father's health and eat a meat roll which my travelling companion refuses, being the practicing vegetarian she is. Outside, police agents armed with submachine guns and bulletproof vests wander around the backstreets with a wary air; but once they have been told why we are there, they smile in amusement, displaying their bright white teeth: "Are you here to take pictures? Yes. And where do you come from? Italy. Ah, Europe, how long does it take? Not much, six hours." Handshakes, warm farewells and long live Pakistan.

Pakistan, Italy, relationships between states, nations founded from one day to the next, looking onto the world; cities to be built from scratch, long lists of departments to organize into offices. Appointments made via telegram from the CDA (Capital Development Agency), to which Ponti, founder of the P.F.R. studio,[9] would respond in the name of the other two members, it must be said, generously: "I have thought over this point that influences my work. On the first option (a single architect designs all the buildings) my opinion is that even were it to be entrusted to a genius, it might detract richness and vital human (and historical) meaning from your capital city; [...] the second alternative I am more in agreement with: of course, it is essential for the coordinator, along with the gifts of an excellent architect, to be endowed with a human and moral understanding of the expressions of other architects, as well as that of being able to summon up all their creative energies. This is as important as there being great respect and regard between the various architects to whom each building is entrusted."[10]

Four hundred kilometers to the east, beyond the high-security border with India, lies a city similar in terms of size and layout, planned in rectangles of a kilometer and a half by seven hundred meters: Chandigarh. According to the guide which I had found in February 1981 at the Mountain View, the hotel where I ended up, and which consists of a rather handmade notebook yet packed full of information: "The layout of the city was designed by Albert Mayer in New York in collaboration with Matthew Novicki. When Novicki died in an aeroplane accident in 1950, the work was entrusted to the famous architect and urbanist Le Corbusier, to his cousin Pierre Jeanneret, and to the English couple Maxwell Fry and Jane B. Drew."[11] I had spent three days wandering around Le Corbusier's buildings, who—as a sixty-three-year-old, finally far from the suffocating Europe—had given the very best of himself. Two years later, my plan had spread to include Louis Kahn's work in Dacca, but I changed my mind at the last minute when the curfew was declared—or at least that was what the papers in Calcutta had said, perhaps confusing a tram set on fire with the opening shots of a revolution in Bangladesh.

Today, along the road from Islamabad to Rawalpindi, the great two-kilometer squares designed by Doxiadis may be seen. Multiplied by six, and then again by two, a rectangular city is

9
P.F.R., initials of the Ponti, Fornaroli, Rosselli Studio, 1952–1979.

10
Gio Ponti, letter to Aktar Mahmood, Secretary of the CDA, Capital Development Authority, August 1961. Epistolario Gio Ponti (Gio Ponti's epistolary), Milan.

11
Chandigarh City of Roses, tourist guide, local publisher, 1980.

created of around thirty square kilometers. Tall buildings along the Kashmir Highway and behind it, in the secondary rows, ever lower constructions as you move away from the east-west

route that ideally leads to Kashmir. In the middle, the train track that goes to Rawalpindi looks like the line in Mexico City, running alongside the motorways that connect it to a boundless territory. "The train isn't used very much because people prefer to move around by car, just like in your country," I am told by Saboohi Sarshar, the architect who accompanies us for a day around Pindi—the local abbreviation, knocking off the "Rawal." Now and then, Saboohi draws up to the pavement and speaks to his collaborators; we Italians exploit the moment to take photographs: oranges heaped up against piles of earth, mosques and dusty parking lots, orange diesel trucks, billboard advertisements for fashionable shoes, rustic butchers, carwashes, and things like that. At a certain point, the railway line rises up on pillars and proceeds above the old town and its roads full of traffic, its inhabitants entirely absorbed in work and various kinds of commerce. The reinforced concrete pillars that hold it up accompany us for miles. We are proceeding at a walking pace towards an otherwise unidentified city center.

An artist and an anthropologist have joined us, and they introduce us to life in the neighborhood in front of a house several storeys high inhabited by the transgender community which has been accepted by the local area and the usually severe Islamic religion. The house allotted to them was originally a highly prestigious building with loggias and windows with inlaid wood from the colonial era, later painted over with bright colors, greens and yellows; a very British solution, deployed not only in London but also in Simla, a heavenly village with a charming name two hours away from Chandigarh, perched on the mountains two thousand feet above sea level. Today home to Pindi's transgender community, apparently uninhabited, it conserves the crumbling memory in its paints. By pure chance, a few meters away from the trans community, the craftsman who sells me an openable brass lotus flower at a rather dear price uses a page from the *The News International* to wrap it up displaying the headline "Trans rights—an elusive dream." A cartoon in the center of the page portrays a girl undecided as to whether to become part of the male world, the female world, or both. On both sides, doctors of different sexes are all too ready to advise her for the best.

And so, just to remind myself of where I am, I turn to the various forms of nostalgia passed on to me by the photographs from sixty years before; my mother Giovanna Ponti is portrayed together with my father on the building site of the Secretariats. They are both standing on an escarpment and, from behind them, the building under construction peeks out. She is dressed elegantly in dark shades, and as she talks to him she accompanies her words with hand gestures; he, with his light-colored raincoat and his hands in his pockets, looks at her and listens, although he seems to be thinking about other things. She is forty years old, he a few years more, and they look like a close couple; in the eyes of their son, the relationship between his parents is always a mystery, with the alternation of dangerous alliances against him and then outbursts of unmotivated approval. The mother, while not abdicating from her role as a connection with life, is always the parent who transmits more to her son: stories, anecdotes that start with the words "Did you know, when we were on our way to Pakistan, passing through Delhi, in the hotel restaurant we would see Alberto Moravia and Pier Paolo Pasolini having dinner? They would talk non-stop, and at a certain point of the evening, when Moravia would go up to his room to sleep, Pasolini would go out in search of adventure"; the closing words tossed in lightly and with calculated malice, she herself a great reader of Pasolini, Carlo Emilio Gadda, Joseph Roth, and fables from all over the world, a traveler and translator for Longanesi of the life of Lauren Bacall, of the two editions of Doctor Spock, both the one in which children have to be cuddled and the later version in which a good smack here and there is advised.

In the days leading up to my departure, I had decided to introduce my lecture at the IAP with a sequence of family photographs: father, mother, grandfather, myself at two years of age in my father's arms, him beaming down on me. The choice was right on the money: the audience of the first lecture at the School of Art and Architecture, 90 percent female (some wearing a headscarf but most with their hair loose), followed the presentation with a degree of curiosity as the history of a dynasty inclined to do nothing but toil away; it's the prelude to the second section of my photographs of quite a different tone: worlds, views from a speeding car, disjointed contemporary architecture by reflections, automobiles, et cetera.

Towards the end, a female student stands up: "What do you think of Instagrammability, the extreme and typically postmodern theory (devised by two Italian scholars)[12] on the adaptation of architecture to its ensuing representation on smartphones?" "Well, in my view, our world produces reams of philosopher-curators who consider the critique of contemporary society to be an actual job (what a bore); a few months ago, a British journalist asked me whether by chance I loathed the architects I photograph. I replied no, I didn't; nevertheless, a professor present at the lecture was of the same opinion..." The student showed she had understood that, when you take photographs, your involvement with the subject is such that you really don't know quite where you'll end up. I came to a conclusion suggesting that, in the case of misunderstandings, "you can always blame your own, perfidious alter ego."

After the brief debate, a moment of peace on the roof of the university; everyone smokes. While people converse with the professors, my mind wanders as I admire the campus below us: a sprawling space with a few well-distanced tower blocks, linked by stone footpaths. It makes you want to stare at the clouds while lying on the grass, which is all yellow due

12
Giulia Pistone
and Fabiola Fiocco,
Strelka Institute,
Moscow, 2019.

to the lack of rain over the last few months. The conversation starts to dry up around the theme of climate change, but luckily someone cites the River Indus. For me, the Indus has been the stuff of fantasy for days, captured on a picture postcard that makes me dream; purchased at the hotel designed by Ponti —the wrong one—it is titled *Indus Boat*, and it portrays a fishing boat with two people on board, seemingly sailing through foam or flurries of snow; the water is the same light blue as the sky, and the estuary of the Indus looks like an ocean.

The sun is low at five in the afternoon as we make our way back towards the city; against the light, we see flocks of sheep and young farmhands with hessian sacks full of hay and other farm produce; they halt the traffic with their hands, smile and make their way through the brushwood on the other side of the motorway; we return their greetings. The scene reminds me of the meeting with a Pakistani architect on a flight from Delhi to Amritsar, I think it was in 1982. He explained to me that the frequent coups in his country didn't worry the peasant population very much, concerned as they were with trade and cattle-farming; politics was a remote problem which concerned only those few who might draw any benefit from it, meaning those in Islamabad.

Over cups of tea and dinner invitations, the conversation frequently shifts from architecture to the current state of Pakistan: I'm intrigued, as it were, by the much talked-about and publicized death sentence for Parvez Musharraf, ex-Prime Minister, widely loved by all for his ability to manage the economy; the sentence was issued ten years after he had left the political stage for misdoings that were not entirely clear. Justice distorting reality and rewriting history is not an entirely new concept to me, and much mirth may be made of judges' willingness to pursue retroactive vendettas; be as it may, "Musharraf lives between Dubai and London," someone at the other end of the table adds; more laughter follows. And so I remind the others that in the days of the P.F.R. studio, mention was often made at home of Ali Bhutto, a wayward leader and modernizer who ended up behind bars and was then sentenced to death through retroactive justice. "Basically, sending ex-leaders to their death seems to be a national sport," I add, almost certain that I wouldn't be hurting anyone's feelings.

The family, on the other hand, is a serious topic, and one that is not only part of the list of unwritten laws, but part of the nervous system of every individual: the mother (or grandmother)

is always held in great consideration; she lives in close contact with her children and grandchildren, as a symbol of continuity. During a dinner, the young and brilliant architect Fawad S. Abbasi explains to me that it was he who went to live with his father, not the other way round as I had imagined. The creator together with his father of extremely elegant buildings, he manages a studio in the same large building where he lives. His wife Amna, a graphic artist, tells of her mother, who lives in Karachi, an extremely hot and uninhabitable place; she has two passports, a Pakistani and a British one. Zahir Uddin Kawayas, an architect who has come from Lahore especially for the occasion, tells of his encounters with Ponti and Rosselli in the 1960s. No longer young, in a blue jacket, accompanied by his three very glamorous daughters and with a perfect English accent, sitting next to me in the car heading towards the restaurant, he has a strong vein of irony running through him: "The prime minister is a total idiot." General approval for his comment, also by the driver, who is trying to steer a Toyota full of architects and photographers between double-parked cars and policemen brandishing shiny automatic weapons and transceivers.

The restaurant has large bookshelves that the diners may access. In front of me, Jahangir Khan Sherpao, an architect of around seventy years of age who studied in Chicago and who is very active in his relations with Asia, asks whether he can interview me after having heard my lecture at the IAP. He is a brilliant fellow, and his calling card bears the word 'CITÉ' in yellow block capitals.

I say yes, but I ask him—with calculated naivety—how an intellectual might couple the contemporary world with the Islamic faith: in fact, before I took to the stage at the IAP venue, a voice boomed forth from the loudspeakers repeating the name of Allah, accompanied by traditional phrases and music; just after that, it was time for the Pakistani national anthem complete with sitar-playing. What's more, at the end of my presentation, Jahangir has asked me which architects I had no respect for, obtaining no more than a smile and a diplomatic answer from me. At that point, in a rare display of humor, he proposed locking the doors to keep my secret, thus putting my back to the wall. The audience laughed a little. I gave in and came up with a few names; the echo of my words withered in the hall, and then Giovanna added her own considerations, which happened to be much along the same lines. Then there was a general wave of relaxation.

Jahangir answers my questions synthetically: Islam is their future and not only their present. I let it go, but the following evening, on being invited by Asad Khan to her very cosy studio, I ask him for clearer information on the difference between Sunnites and Shiites, something which has always provoked serious comprehension problems. At that point, Giovanna glares at me desperately from behind her mobile phone with which she is following her team in Milan, foreseeing that the answer will carry on for hours. And soon after, I myself—on hearing of cousins, wives, and whole families in disagreement—feel lost, and so shift the conversation towards topics more firmly within my grasp.

Futile yet profound observations a few days later, one of the last if I'm not wrong, when everyone was a little sad for the farewells to be given. It's a nice day, and the afternoon sun shines straight into our eyes. We are in a tourist enclave that brings together family entertainment areas, open-air museums, a Hindu temple, and a fabric bazaar. Asad Khan reminds us that the idea for this village was that of the lamented Musharraf. There are three good-looking girls sitting near us in high heels and European-style attire. In hushed tones, I share my observations with Giovanna; she points out that the area is occupied by little groups of women and men, sitting at tables at a distance from one another like in a game of chess. It's true: I had picked up on a detail but without taking in the general picture, i.e. this strategy of establishing contact between men and women in a still rather traditionalist country.

Shortly before, at the entrance to the village, a tightrope walker with a gray jacket had welcomed us with a very cute monkey in a tiny outfit on a little chain. Having seen monkeys in action more than once, and how quickly they can steal food from the shopping bags of slightly dopey British tourists (despite the fact that exotic travel is very much part of their DNA), I kept to a safe distance. Behind the tightrope-walker/monkey couple, a huge and garish poster reminds visitors of the friendship between the people of Pakistan and China. And to make it more authoritative, it features the founding fathers, Ali Jinnah and Mao Zedong. It is hand-painted, and the artist made the hands of the two presidents very similar, although the jacket sleeve underlines the differences between the cultures: one embellished with colorful embroidery, the Communist one entirely plain.

We embark on a brief visit around a museum set up in an open-air space under a portico: our host is the son of a local politician who had brought together images from the birth of Pakistan and put them into chronological order, positioning them on the basis of the importance of the figures portrayed. It starts from group photographs of architects in shirtsleeves, in the open, trousers flapping in the wind which blows up clouds of dust; in one shot at sunset (also featuring the long shadow cast by the photographer) there is also Doxiadis, the big boss over from Greece, although it's hard to pick him out in the midst of some thirty other architects. Also the female delegation visiting from Lahore is rather numerous, having their photo taken as they smile before a bare landscape in the bright midday sun; behind them we can make out a sprawling plain hosting various plantations.

In the images, the politicians, military men, and big players stand out thanks to their apparel: one of them is digging for the laying of the first stone; in the following image, there are two of them no less planting a sapling, one digging with a spanking new shovel while the other holds a dwarf eucalyptus in his hand. The ceremony is presided over by Farah Palavi, a fascinating woman surrounded by security guards. Judging by the expressions of those present, the dig would appear to be interminable. But it's all justifiable: the operation is not an easy one on the sun-scorched terrain. Without fail, the truly powerful always wear sunglasses even to evening press conferences: their faces captured with close-up flashes are serious and their gazes impenetrable, without so much as the hint of a smile. In order to compare the backgrounds and the landscapes that I have in front of me, I find a photo of Ponti and Rosselli on my phone in a mosque in the 1960s: they too are in shirtsleeves (it's clearly very hot) and have footwear generally used for religious reasons. They look embarrassed at the photographer having caught them unawares and are mustering a half-smile. I turn off my mobile phone.

I move a meter, in front of the framed portrait of the first president of Pakistan, Ayub Khan, admiring the construction of Islamabad through binoculars: his bushy black moustache make him look a lot like Saddam Hussein. In the next panel, Jinnah, the father-inventor of Pakistan, has a fragile and emaciated air to him, no longer that of the wealthy British gentleman who resides in an elegant Anglo-Indian style dwelling. A pity that a good-looking man like him is handed down to posterity in such an evanescent and clearly touched up image. But the day of the inauguration of the Secretariats is a national holiday, and President Khan passes among the crowds in his Cadillac along a dirt track; the buildings are depicted in color photographs with pools full of gushing water and gardens laid out in Moghul style, even though in actual fact they are not. In another frame, the red double-decker London buses may be seen, ready to transport the passengers who would soon come to occupy the Secretariats of Islamabad. I look at the photograph of a bus which is about to go under a bridge. Hopefully, the driver has already calculated the height and it is not about to charge headlong into a block of concrete. We thank our young museum owner for this pleasant journey through the recent past of Islamabad. We reach our table and start to swap the various dishes as citizens of the world: carnivores and vegetarians, the secularized and the believers.

ISLAMABAD
TODAY

ISLAMABAD TODAY
OCTOBER, 1968

Published by :	PUBLIC RELATIONS DIRECTORATE, CAPITAL DEVELOPMENT AUTHORITY, ISLAMABAD.
Edited by :	MAJ. ZAMIR JAFRI, TQA. S. A. T. WASTI.
Printed at	KHURSHEED PRINTERS, ISLAMABAD.

CONTENTS

Foreword : Lieut-General K. M. Sheikh.	i
The Project and Perspective.	1
Site Selection Commission.	2
The Site	4
Federal Capital Commission.	5
Capital Development Authority.	7
The Curtain Rises.	8
Regional Planning.	9
The Plan and the Planning.	11
The Architecture.	15
Landscaping.	17
Rehabilitation Task.	23
Municipal Administration.	25
Medical Services.	26
Roads and Bridges.	27
Water Supply, Sewage and Drainage.	28
Major Buildings.	30
Mosques.	38
Some Other Buildings.	39
Basic Information.	42
Progress at a Glance.	43

On the western side of this first thoroughfare, auxiliary services are to be put in place, considered part of Rawalpindi, while on the eastern side, cultural installations are foreseen.

THE PROJECT AND THE PERSPECTIVE

The story of Islamabad goes back to 1947

The new sovereign state of Pakistan came into being on August 14, 1947. The Central Government of the new State had to be hurriedly shifted from Delhi to somewhere in Pakistan, and, under the circumstances, Karachi was then the only city where it could go. It was, however, a purely temporary arrangement to establish a bridge-head. The need to have a proper Capital was in the mind of the people and the Government. The Central Government had no permanent home of its own.

Though a new country we, as a people, are an old nation, with a rich heritage. Inspired by a historical past, and keen to build a dignified present and a great future, the people naturally were eager to build a new city. Successive Governments gave their thoughts to the question of Capital building. Even a number of sites like Mauripur, Gizri and Gadap were considered but for one reason or the other the project was never pursued determinedly. In 1958, when President Ayub came to the helm and the country achieved political stability and economic progress, this important national task was also taken up in the right earnest.

ew of new two-storey houses under construction in sector G-7

A two-storey, multifamily house.

The Curtain Rises

The task was to create a City of hopes and aspirations. To create right environments, to quote from President Ayub's famous book "Friends Not Masters" "to provide light and direction to the efforts of people". To create a City which should be symbol of our unity, our national identity; a Capital from which would flow the inspiration which pulsates life into the nation. It was a big task. It was a big opportunity as well.

The curtain rose with the constitution of Capital Development Authority commissioned to make all arrangements for the development and construction of the City.

The Master Plan provided only an outline and a broad frame of concepts and criteria. The beginning of a series of complex problems started in actual implementation. It involved interpretation of principles and their application on the ground, fitting in all details with the abstract criteria, marriage of physical conditions with the principles, adjustment of standards and resources, relationship between values and systems, in short the task of development and enforcement within the discipline of the Plan.

It was in October, 1961, that the construction work commenced and the first digging was made on the ground in what is now commonly known as the Aab-Para neighbourhood. Exactly after two years in October 1963, the City began to walk and talk.

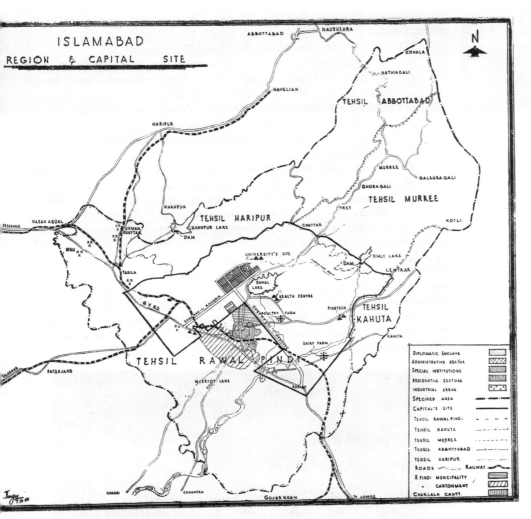

ISLAMABAD
REGION & CAPITAL SITE

N

The framework of the federal area is completed through the positioning of a second perpendicular road which follows the orientation of the landscape, running parallel to the hills.

Regional Planning

The Islamabad Region, extending from Kohala, Nathiagali, Ayubia to the southern boundary of Rawalpindi Tehsil and from the eastern

The intersection between these two main roads is known today as Zero Point.

boundary of Rawalpindi Tehsil to Hassan Abdal, covers an area of 1,400 square miles.

The main objectives of the Regional Plan are :-

a) An integrated programme of development in the field of agriculture, industry, social and environmental conditions, formulated within the scope and capabilities of the region and national policy influencing such developments;

b) An optimum distribution of population in the rural and urban areas according to a well-planned pattern of urban and rural settlements; and

c) Coordinated programme of development of urban and rural communities to reduce intra-regional differences in living standards and imbalances between urban and rural communities.

After making the research design, a study was carried out in order to determine the size, type and distribution of settlements. Factors which have led to the rise or decline of settlements were also examined. A preliminary report has recently been completed. Field investigations have been made and a detailed Socio-Economic Survey would be carried out in order to find out the existing conditions. On the basis of the information thus collected, the Regional Plan would be prepared. It is expected that this plan, which would serve as a guide line for future activity, would be ready within a year.

President Field Marshal Mohammad Ayub Khan inspecting the Secretariat Blocks in March, 1967.

10

Mr. Edward D. Stone explaining the model of the President's House to the high-level Govt. Design Committee. Photo shows (from right to left) Mr. Ghiasuddin Ahmed, Defence Secretary, Mr. T.G. Nasir Khan, Additional Secretary, Finance; Mr. M. H. Sufi, Cabinet Secretary; Mr. N. A. Faruqui, Chief Election Commissioner; Mr. M. M. Ahmad, Deputy Chairman, Planning Commission; Mr. S. Fida Hasan, Adviser to the President; Gen. K. M. Sheikh, Chairman, CDA; and Mr. S. A. M. Khan, Works Secretary, (fourth from left).

The Plan and the Planning

The urbanisation of Islamabad is based on the principle of 'dyna-polis that is to say a mobile arrangement which grows in scale and size smoothly and coherently with all the functions of city life, at all stages of development, the city-centre moving proportionately to the movement of the residential sectors.

Each sector is a self-contained township, satisfying sector's needs. While it takes care of all the requirements of modernity, it ensures at the same time the traditional character of the neighbourhood, serving the residents at the human level and enabling them to live comfortably in happier surroundings. There is no discrimination in the matter of services and facilities. Unity of the city as a whole would be achieved through detailed zoning regulations, framed to exercise control on town-planning and architecture.

FUNCTIONAL ZONES

The city is divided into various functional zones which broadly are :

i) **The Administrative Sector.**

This sector is located towards the north-east and is situated on the main axis of the city. It will contain principal public buildings like the President's House, the Secretariat Blocks, the National Assembly Building, the Supreme Court, the Plan House (Headquarters of the Planning Commission) and a group of cultural buildings. The designs of the National Archives, and the National Museum Building, prepared by Sir Robert Matthew of U.K., have been finalised. The Administrative Sector would form the most focal complex of the metropolitan city. This sector has already come to life with the shifting of the Ministries to the permanent Secretariat buildings. The Central Square, the heart of Islamabad

11

comprising the National Assembly Building, the President's House, the Foreign Office and Cabinet Division block is expected to start throbbing by 1970. A befitting National War Memorial would also be erected here to perpetuate the memory of those officers and men of the Pakistan Armed Forces who made the supreme sacrifice in defence of the Country during the September, 1965 War against India.

ii) **Diplomatic Enclave.**

The special enclave for the chanceries and residences of the foreign missions is situated in a very pleasant setting, close to the picturesque Rawal Lake. With an average elevation of 1800 feet above sea level, its gentle slopes lend themselves to the construction of interesting buildings at various levels. A small stream meanders through the area. Some of the countries who purchased land have started construction work on the site.

(Left) An Embassy building under construction the Diplomatic Enclave. (Below) State Bank bu under construction in Special Buildings Area.

iii) **Special Buildings Area :** Bordering the Administrative Sector and the Diplomatic Enclave is a special buildings area, meant for hotels, banks and other public and City buildings. The buildings of the Hotel Shahrazad, the Government Hostel, Telephone and Telegraph Exchange and the 11-storey State Bank of Pakistan (fast nearing completion) are located in this area.

iv) **The Residential Sectors.**

The residential sectors have been planned in rows, placed on both sides of the main civic, commerce and business centre which runs in the heart of the town. The area of each residential sector is 1.25 square miles and the plots vary in size from 600 to 2,000 square yards. Each sector is, in itself a self-contained and self-sufficient township. A sector is again sub-divided into several smaller residential neighbourhoods which are served by various grades of community centres, equipped with

12

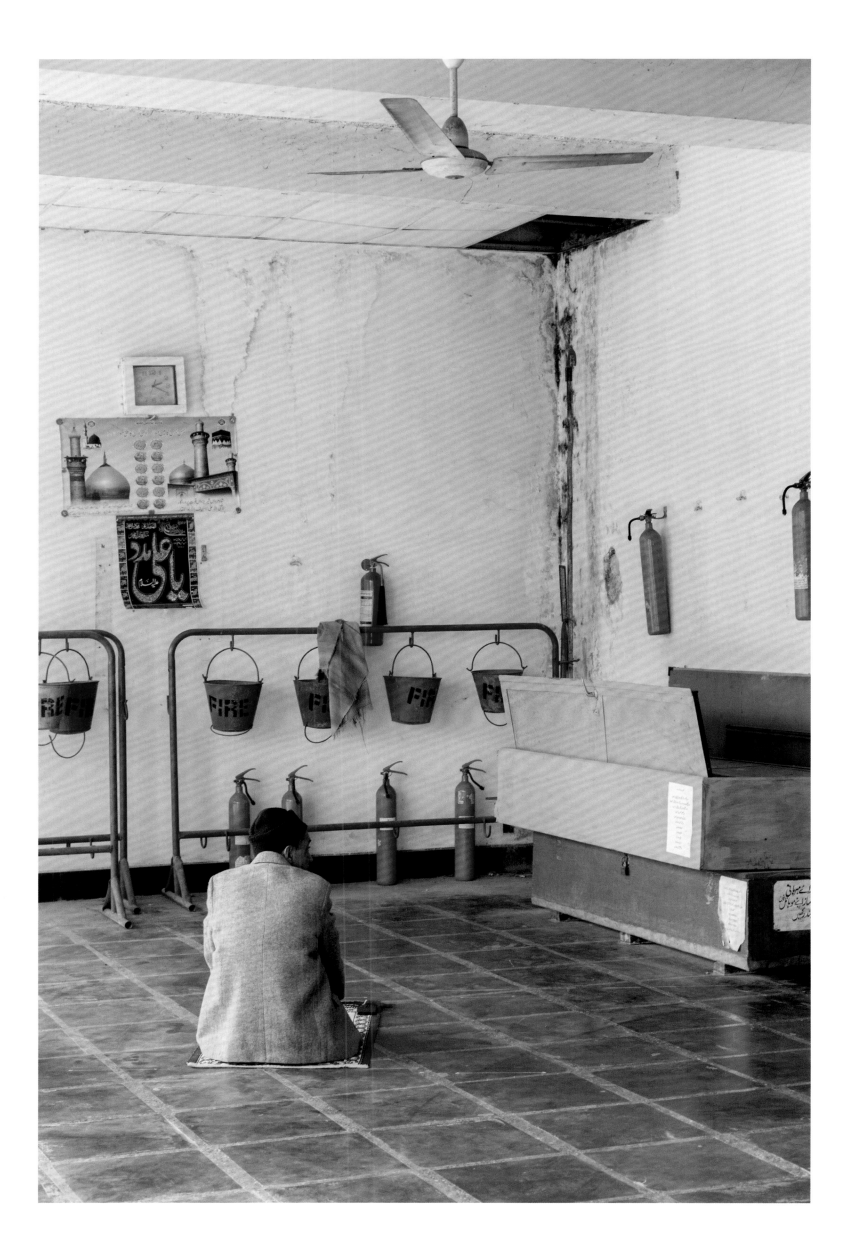

Cinema, shops and bank in a residential sector

civic facilities and services like schools, mosques, markets, dispensaries, play-grounds, parks, etc., according to their requirements. The main community centre of a sector will have offices for local services, higher educational institutions, the sectoral post office, hospital, police station, cinema house, club and large departmental shops and store houses. This civic hierarchy is repeated more or less in each sector. The emphasis has been on the provision of facilities and services almost at the doorstep.

v) **Blue Area :** The main Civic, Commerce and Business Zone, which is at present commonly known as the Blue Area runs through the heart of the City in between the residential Sectors. It would have Offices, Banks, Insurance Companies, business houses and big departmental stores. The spacious Capital Avenue which forms the ceremonial

13

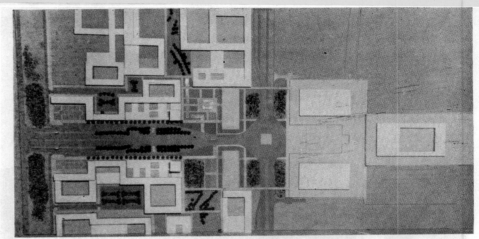

Model showing a section of the Blue Area.

approach to the Central Square, passes through this area. The lay-out of this area of multi-storeyed, impressive buildings has been revised to further enlarge its utility and aesthetic dimension. Zoning regulations, too, have been realistically modified.

vi) The National Park.

A vast valley spread over an area of about 188 square miles is earmarked as the National Park Area. The institutions of national importance such as the Atomic Research Institute and the National Health Laboratories are already functioning in this area. Institutions, requiring large areas of land would be located in this area. It would also have spacious sports centre, parks and exhibition grounds. Agricultural, dairy. and poultry farms have also been located in this area. Recently, its functional scope has been enlarged to include establishment of a few Model Villages, at suitable places to facilitate the settlement of the displaced families near their ancestoral surroundings as far as possible.

The 2000-foot high Shakarparian Hill is also located in this area and serves as a vantage point. It gives a panoramic view of the city.

vii) Green Belt.

About a mile wide green belt has been provided to emphasize a natural green demarcation between the Cities of Islamabad and Rawalpindi. The area would also be utilised for location of academic, cultural and social institutions. At present the buildings of the Degree College, Islamabad, the Inter-University Board and the Poly-technic stand in this belt.

viii) The Industrial Zones.

Two separate zones for the location of manufacturing and light service industry have been established. The manufacturing industry zone, located in close proximity to Rawalpindi will enable the industries to serve both Islamabad and Rawalpindi and also to draw the labour force. Properly laid out labour colonies have also been planned in the vicinity.

Light service industries and handicrafts with its own retail have been located in a belt on the two-lane Service Road skirting the southern edge of the residential sectors. Both zones are today humming with the construction activity and a large number of commercial and industrial units have gone into production.

14

In Doxiadis' view, Rawalpindi must facilitate the development of the new capital; he elaborates a masterplan with the aim of separating functions between the two twin urban areas.

Gen. K.M. Sheikh, Chairman, CDA, explaining the system evolved by C.D.A. to name various localities and various grades of roads in Islamabad; to the Design Committee appointed by the Govt. Photo shows from (left to right) Mr. Asghar Hussain Raza, Financial Adviser, C.D.A.; Mr. Qudratullah Shahab, Education Secretary; Mr. M.H. Sufi, Cabinet Secretary; Mr. Altaf Gauhar, Information Secretary; Mr. T.G. Nasir Khan, Additional Secretary, Finance; and Col. Muhammad Nawaz Khan, Member Administration, C.D.A.

THE ARCHITECTURE

Building a new Capital is indeed a rare and memorable event in the history of nations. Within the current century there have been only a few examples of national Capitals being built, notable among them being New Delhi, Canberra, and Chandigarh.

Pattern of architecture was obviously a question of great concern. The complexity of the problem does not lie in its functional aspect; it is in the historical and cultural dimensions. The question was: shall we make a clean break with the past and make something completely new or shall we adopt the traditional designs.

The problem was carefully studied. Experts were consulted; seminars were held. We have a rich heritage of traditional architecture. But the flow and growth of the traditions have, unfortunately, been blocked by a lengthy gap of alien domination. We are building Islamabad in the 20th Century. Concepts, mode and method of architecture have undergone radical changes. Technology has advanced tremendously. We,

15

The two cities will share the airport in Chaklala and Rawal Lake, as well as highway and railway communications.

as a people, have accepted the universal criteria in the way of life, the functioning of administration, conference and residences, and the provision of modern amenities such as air-conditioning, elevators etc. Our architects and engineers, too, have been educated and trained in the modern methods. The skill and the materials necessarily required to achieve traditional effects are not available.

The question was examined in all its dimensions and after careful deliberations it was resolved that architecture should reflect a high-minded simplicity, economy and utility that is both purposeful and graceful and not wasteful or ostentatious, that fullest possible advantage should be taken of modern research and materials, that landscape and natural beauty should be carefully preserved and treated, and that shapes and designs should be evolved for functional as well as aesthetic satisfaction.

The endeavour, therefore, should be towards evolution of architecture in a progressive manner commensurate with the ability of the national resources and talents to find the designs which will have to be a compromise, blending the traditional and modern concepts of architecture and the local and the universal criteria into a workable and pleasing totality. Every building is to have an individuality, no doubt, but it must fit in with the overall urban design.

Having taken this basic decision the next question was directly connected with the achievement of an architectural unity in the main Capital Complex and the city as a whole. There were various approaches to this problem which had been tried out by other countries. In the most recent example such as Brazilia and Chandigarh the governments had entrusted the entire designing of all major buildings to one prominent architect. The Capital Development Authority, however, adopted, after a detailed examination, a new approach of achieving unity through the concerted efforts of a co-ordinated panel of world-famous architects whose work was basically in sympathy with each other. This method, it was felt, would impart variety and vigour to the architectural conception without destroying the essential unity. It would also avoid repetition of architectural cliches. The work of these architects, however, was to be mainly confined to the major buildings.

In the field of Government Housing CDA has itself prepared a large number of designs for the houses of Government servants of various income groups starting from the lowest paid staff. These designs could also be made available to the private individuals on nominal cost. The aim in these designs has been to provide the minimum accommodation of 2 rooms even for the lowest paid Government servant and a graduated scale of higher accommodation for other Government servants. Adequate out-door living-space is a particular feature of all low-cost housing. It is perhaps for the first time that two rooms have been provided in the houses of peons and other similar staff, fitted with modern amenities, including Gas. It may also be mentioned here that peons and similar staff get rent-free accommodation.

The process of research and experimentation is constantly kept under focus. Pakistani Architects are commissioned to design housing projects. Recently, in 1968, a Directorate of Architecture has been established to further emphasise the architectural aspect. In the Government Housing Sector, a door-to-door survey has recently been conducted to obtain views of the occupants in the light of living experience.

The approach seeks to obtain a happy blending of the social values, traditional spirit with the modern idiom, taking the fullest advantage of modern research and technology. Islamabad thus provides a new approach to architecture in Pakistan, and, it is hoped, its tremendous impact will be reflected in the architecture of the country.

16

GOVERNMENT PRINTING PRESS

LANDSCAPING

The landscape development is an integral part of the modern town planning. Structures, however, mighty and magnificent may be, do not attain a pleasing look without proper landscaping. It is a serious and specialised skill which combines the knowledge of the geographer, the botanist, the horticulturist, with dreams and visions of the artist. It is a continuation and an extension of architecture into the realm of outdoor space.

Gardens and parks have an immense functional, recreational and aesthetic value. A city without them is a city without the environment which enhances the value and meaning of life. As a nation, we have a rich and picturesque heritage in this aesthetic field.

Landscaping aspect has been duly emphasized throughout Islamabad. Landscape architects and horticulturists have been working together from the outset to ensure an attractive and wholesome environment to human life in the Capital City.

17

Islamabad will grow, but in only one direction: in a parabolic fashion.

On reaching a certain stage of development, the capital will absorb Rawalpindi within its own metropolitan area.

MAJOR BUILDINGS

President's House

The President's House, planned to be built on a complex of three hills, will form the central and predominant core of the Administrative Sector. Standing atop 2,000 ft. hill, terminating the vista along the monumental Capital Avenue, it will command an extensive panoramic view of the surroundings.

While driving along this avenue one will be looking straight into the President's House. Flanking the Central Square on the south and north will be the National Assembly and the Cabinet Secretariat and Foreign Office buildings.

The building has been designed by Mr. Edward D. Stone, a renowned Architect. Mr. Tajuddin M. Bhamani and Company, are his Pakistani Associates in the project. The design has been approved by the Government Design Committee and the development of the site has already commenced.

The Presidential Estate would accommodate all its necessary domestic, social and administrative elements. The public portion will have the President's Secretariat and a spacious Cabinet room. It will also have reception and banquet hall for public functions and suites for the State guests. The President's Secretariat and the residence will be connected with collonades on both sides with a traditional Moghul Garden laid out in between. A mosque has also been provided within the premises.

Although the building will be modern in all aspects, care has been taken to achieve a traditional architectural touch by the judicious use of jalies, fountains and gardens.

30

National Assembly

The National Assembly Building will constitute an important feature in the most focal complex of the buildings like the President's House and the Cabinet Secretariat and Foreign Office Blocks planned to be built around the ceremonial Central Square. The complex has been rhythmically harmonised with the surroundings. Architecturally it would be an engaging structure.

The schematic design, prepared by Mr. Edward D. Stone, has already been approved by the high-level Government Committee appointed to scrutinise designs of major public buildings to be built in Islamabad and work on the detailed drawings is in progress.

With a circular form Chamber, the building has architecturally been conceived to portray the orderly character of traditional idioms.

The main chamber will also serve as a venue for international conferences. A flexible arrangement of seats has been conceived to ensure 1500 capacity in case of big international gatherings.

Provision has been made for special boxes for the President and the Speaker. Adequate arrangements have also been made for distinguished visitors, and galleries for the Press and public committee rooms, offices of the Ministers. division lobbies, lounges, and restaurants etc. In addition to a prayer hall utility services like post and telegraph, bookshop, travel agency and banking facilities will also be available. The Secretariat of the National Assembly and some elements of the Parliamentary Affairs Division will also be located in the building.

31

The aims of the government and those of Doxiadis do not always coincide: the military regime wants an isolated central administration.

Islamabad   University

The Islamabad University, a unitary type, fully residential and post-graduate institution is being built over an area of 1500 acres. The foundation stone of the University was laid by President Field Marshal Mohammad Ayub Khan, on June 21, 1967.

The site is located to the east of the Secretariat Buildings, near the base of Margalla Hills, in a picturesque setting. The terrain is semi-hilly and rolling. The site affords beautiful vistas on all sides and overlooks Rawal Lake towards south.

Designed by Mr. Edward D. Stone, the plan reflects the natural land characteristics of the site, the micro-climate and a special organization of structural forms that promulgate the educational programme precepts. The functional relationship of the various institutes, the Central Core and ancillary facilities were carefully studied to achieve an optimum ease of interdisciplinary movement with ready access to the general use facilities. The Campus Core Buildings have been strategically placed among the Institutes to form a strong axial spine with the Library in the centre. The master plan and the type of building designed by the architect have ample scope to meet all such future expansion needs.

The work on construction of three hostel blocks is already in progress. The construction of another five buildings is expected to commence soon.

Islamabad University Hostel under construction.

32

MAJOR BUILDINGS (COMPLETED)

Secretariat Blocks

Rising like a massive fortress against the Margalla backdrop, the Secretariat Blocks present a robustly pleasant panorama in harmony with the natural environment. Entering the vast complex the eye is caught by sharp angular blocks.

To house the Central Government in Islamabad, the Secretariat Buildings, with built-up area of one million square feet, are located in

33

the north-eastern half of the Administrative Sector. The multi-storeyed blocks, rising from six to eight storeys including the basement, have been laid out into two groups, each consisting of five interconnected wings or blocks. The system is interwoven with roads, paths and lawns. The terraced gardens with water channels and fountains lend it an overall traditional elegance. The construction work on Phase I started in April, 1963 and the buildings were occupied towards the end of 1966. Work on the other group (Phase II) was commenced in July, 1963 and the blocks were occupied in different stages, from October, 1967 to September, 1968.

The detailed architectural and structural plans of the complex were prepared by the well-known Ponti, Fornarolli and Rosselli group of architects from Milan, Italy. While planning the Secretariat following considerations were emphasized :—

i) Maximum utilization of the built-up area.
ii) Placement of units to ensure efficiency and flexibility to permit adjustments for occasional re-arrangement in the structure and the distribution of Ministries.
iii) Creation of an appropriate architecture and environment for the functionaries.

Structurally the buildings are designed in reinforced cement concrete frame structure, based on the modern concept of modular planning. A special feature of the plan is the arrangement of entrances at different levels to avoid overcrowding. Due regard has also been kept of the climatic conditions and the movement of the sun during various seasons of the year and different times of the day. Provision has also been made for committee rooms, record rooms, visitors' rooms, messenger rooms and resident clerk's rooms. Services like; Telephone

Secretariat Buildings (Phase II) Four Blocks housing offices of Central Ministries

34

Exchange, Transformer rooms, air-conditioning plant rooms, Post Offices, banks, cycle stands and cafetarias etc., are located on the ground floor and the basement. Four spacious cafetarias have also been provided on the ground floors.

The interior planning of the building has been so designed that connected functions are grouped together to facilitate quick disposal. Modern facilities which are essential and conducive to congenial working of the offices have also been provided.

AIR-CONDITIONING :

Islamabad has extreme climatic conditions both in summer and winter. Cooling of rooms in summer and heating in winter is, therefore, necessary. The studies carried out by the C.D.A. indicated that although the initial cost of central air-conditioning is more than the conventional methods of heating and cooling, but in the long run it is cheaper because of lesser running and operational costs. The buildings have, therefore, been provided with year-round air-conditioning based on natural gas.

Each block has four lifts in a common RCC shaft placed centrally in the building. All lifts are attendant operated but can be key-switched to automatic control, if necessary. These lifts have all modern features of safety and elegance.

Electrification represents the most modern system. The furniture provided, though simple and functional in design, is graceful aesthetically.

Utmost care is being taken to ensure proper maintenance of the buildings. The maintenance aspect has been further emphasised by creation of an exclusive 'service cell' under a Comptroller, who works in close co-ordination with the Ministries and Divisions occupying the blocks.

Moghul Garden, Secretariat Blocks.

35

In the plan, the city appears to be separated from the administrative quarters where the government buildings and ministries are based.

The result is a hybrid plan
of the capital which physically
embodies that dangerous
void in relationships between
institutions and the general
population, to this day a key
feature of Pakistani society.

Hotel

The imposing six storeyed building which now houses the Hotel
Shahrazad, was the first major building to rise in Islamabad. It was
originally commissioned to service in June 1964 with the name of the
Pakistan House. Later on, however, its functional role was changed to
provide a Hotel of international standard in the city. Designed by well
known Italian Architect Gio Ponti, the building consists of 275 rooms.
Residential suites are located in the upper storeys, each storey having 55
units in two rows, connected by a corridor. The Banquet Hall, Committee
rooms, and services and facilities have been located on the ground floor.
The floors are paved with Peshawar marble while on the walls Quetta
onyx has been used with smart ingenuity to suggest as though the stone-
slabs are abstract paintings.

Moghul-style garden in the five-wing Government Hostel.

Government Hostel

Situated in the public buildings area near the Hotel Shahrazad, the still waters of the Government Hostel trickle in cold streams. The main courtyard is half masonary, half garden, where small ornamental trees grow among concrete walks and marble seats. The building is primarily meant for the Members of the National Assembly during the Assembly Session and Government officers visiting Islamabad on temporary duty Residential accommodation is provided in the spacious five wings planned around three quadrangles. Sandy-coloured brick work is headed by fringes of curving white eaves, and on the outside, the balcony and each room is screened by delicate, lace-like concrete. There are in all 138 residential units of which 108 are single rooms and 30 two-room suites. Kitchen facilities are available with the two-room suites and 8 single rooms. All units have attached baths and dressing.

The rooms contain all the conveniences of a modern apartment in the natural delight outside. The view in every direction is one of greenness, with the Rawal Lake glinting on one horizon. From the front the low profile of the building is half-way broken by a vertical tower, of that same hexagonal brick work which decorates the balconies.

Central heating in the rooms and running hot water have been provided in the toilets and kitchennettes. The kitchennettes are also fitted with gas and gas burners. The windows in the rooms are so designed that window type air-conditioners can be easily installed, if required.

Mughal Gardens coupled with extensive use of jali and arched roofs impart an oriental touch to the building.

Photographs
Giovanna Silva

Text
Paolo Rosselli

Copy Editing
Chiara Carpenter

Translation
Bennett Bazalgette-Staples

Proofreading
Agnese Cantelmi (Mousse)

Publishing Editor
Ilaria Bombelli (Mousse)

Publication Design
Massimiliano Pace (Mousse)

© 2021 Mousse Publishing,
the artist, the author of the text

First edition: 2021

Printed in Italy
Intergrafica Verona S.r.l.

ISBN: 978-88-6749-457-6
EUR 25 / USD 29.95

Published and distributed by
Mousse Publishing
Contrappunto s.r.l.
Corso di Porta Romana 63
20122, Milan–Italy

Available through:
Mousse Publishing, Milan
    moussepublishing.com
DAP | Distributed Art Publishers,
New York
    artbook.com
Vice Versa Distribution, Berlin
    viceversaartbooks.com
Les presses du réel, Dijon
    lespressesdureel.com
Antenne Books, London
    antennebooks.com

Paolo Rosselli and Giovanna Silva wish to thank all their friends in
Islamabad who made this work possible:
Fauzia Asad Khan, President of the IAP (Institute of Architects Pakistan)
Jahangir Khan Sherpao, Architect
Salman Javaid Malik, Architect
Fawad Suhail Abbasi, Architect
Amna Majid, Graphic Designer
Umer Iqbal, Architect
Saboohi Sarshar, Architect
Ibtisam A. Peerzada, Capital Development Authority
Nadeem Omar, Center for Culture & Development
Jawwad Zahidi, School of Art, Design & Architecture, Islamabad
Wakar Zaheer Uddin Khawaya, Architect, Lahore
Ahmed Zaid Khan, Professor at ULB, Belgium

Special thanks also go to Stefano Pontecorvo, Italian Ambassador in
Islamabad, to Francesco Gargano, and to the entire staff of the Italian
Embassy in Islamabad.

The historical photographs and reproductions from Pakistani magazines were
kindly provided by the Alberto Rosselli Archive, Milan.